Helping Friends and Family

Taking Care of Others

BY ALYSSA KREKELBERG

The Child's World®
childsworld.com

Published by The Child's World®
1980 Lookout Drive • Mankato, MN 56003-1705
800-599-READ • www.childsworld.com

Photographs ©: SDI Productions/iStockphoto,
cover, 1, 17, 18, 21; Shutterstock Images, 5, 6,
9; Predrag Images/iStockphoto, 10, 13, 14

ISBN 9781503844490 (Reinforced Library Binding)
ISBN 9781503846807 (Portable Document Format)
ISBN 9781503847996 (Online Multi-user eBook)
LCCN 2019956600

Printed in the United States of America

ABOUT THE AUTHOR

**Alyssa Krekelberg is a
children's book editor
and author. She lives
in Minnesota with her
hyper husky.**

Contents

CHAPTER ONE

Helping Someone

Paula falls down while she is walking. She **injures** her leg.

Jane is Paula's granddaughter. Jane is walking a few steps behind with her mom. They see Paula fall. They **rush** over to help.

When a person falls, they can get bruises or even broken bones.

It is important to take care of people when they are hurt.

Jane sees that her grandma's face is scrunched in pain. She is frowning. Jane thinks about a time when she fell on the playground. It hurt a lot.

Paula has a hard time standing up on her own. "Can you help me up?" Paula asks.

Jane does not want her grandma to be in pain. Jane and her mom help Paula up. Jane asks her grandma if she is OK. Paula smiles and says yes.

Paula and Jane walk through the park together. Paula is glad her family members take care of her. Jane is glad, too.

Talk with people who are hurt. Ask if they are OK and if they need your help.

Think about how you would feel if you were sick or hurt.

CHAPTER TWO

Getting Sick

Ken's mom is sick. She **coughs** and sneezes. She has a fever. This means that her body is too warm.

Ken remembers a time when he was sick. His throat hurt and he stayed home from school.

Ken's mom takes care of him when he is sick, which makes him feel better. Ken wants to help his mom, too. He gives her a cup of water to help with her cough.

When someone asks for help, listen closely to what he or she needs.

How can you help someone when he or she is sick?

14

Ken stays by his mom and asks what she needs. Ken's mom is glad that Ken is taking care of her.

THINK ABOUT IT!

Think about a time when someone needed help. Did you help the person? Why or why not? How did that make you feel?

Why is it important to take care of people?

CHAPTER THREE

New Student

Bethany rides the school bus every morning. One morning, a new student joins her. "What is your name?" Bethany asks.

"Allie," she says.

Bethany looks at Allie. She sees that something is wrong. Allie hides her face and cries.

What can you do if
someone near you is sad?

17

Listening to someone talk can help you understand how that person is feeling.

18

"Why are you sad?" Bethany asks.

Allie says that today is her first day at her new school. She is **worried** about making friends.

Bethany listens to Allie because she wants to help Allie feel better.

"You can play with me!" Bethany says.
When they get to school, Bethany
introduces Allie to her other friends.
Allie smiles and thanks Bethany because
she does not feel worried anymore.

Friends take care of each other.

GLOSSARY

coughs (KOFFS) Someone coughs when he or she makes a loud noise from their throat, usually while sick. Ken's mom coughs and sneezes.

injures (IN-jurz) If a person injures herself, that means she is hurt. Paula injures her leg when she falls.

introduces (in-truh-DOOS-es) When someone presents one person to another so they know each other's names, that person introduces them. Bethany introduces Allie to her friends.

rush (RUSH) To rush is to move quickly. Jane and her mom rush to help Paula.

worried (WUR-eed) If someone is concerned about something, that person is worried. Allie was worried about her first day at school.

Books

Dinmont, Kerry. *Dan's First Day of School: A Book about Emotions*. Mankato, MN: The Child's World, 2018.

DiOrio, Rana. *What Does It Mean to Be Present?* Naperville, IL: Little Pickle Press, 2017.

Llenas, Anna. *The Color Monster: A Story about Emotions*. New York, NY: Little, Brown and Company, 2018.

Websites

Visit our website for links about taking care of others:
childsworld.com/links

Note to Parents, Teachers, and Librarians: We routinely verify our Web links to make sure they are safe and active sites. So encourage your readers to check them out!

INDEX